College Success Tips for Adult Learners

PETERSON'S

A  COMPANY

PETERSON'S

A **ⓝelnet.** COMPANY

About Peterson's, a Nelnet company

Peterson's (www.petersons.com) is a leading provider of education information and advice, with books and online resources focusing on education search, test preparation, and financial aid. Its Web site offers searchable databases and interactive tools for contacting educational institutions, online practice tests and instruction, and planning tools for securing financial aid. Peterson's serves 110 million education consumers annually.

For more information, contact Peterson's, 2000 Lenox Drive, Lawrenceville, NJ 08648; 800-338-3282; or find us on the World Wide Web at www.petersons.com/about.

ISBN-13: 978-0-7689-1140-4
ISBN-10: 0-7689-1140-0

Printed in Canada

10   9   8   7   09   08   07

Contents

Introduction

You decided to go to college (or to go back to college); however, you have questions. What are the different types of colleges? How do you get into the mindset of being a student? If you have been away from the classroom for a while, *College Success Tips for Adult Learners* will provide the advice and resources you need to help ease you back into the world of learning.

College Success Tips for Adult Learners sets you on your way and provides easy-to-use information to help you with the decisions you will need to make in order to select a college or program that is right for you. Once you begin your studies, you will find that the book includes great tips for taking exams, writing term papers, and making presentations. There are also study tactics that help you to stay on top of your courses and to manage your time effectively.

You will soon join the ranks of the thousands of adult learners in the United States. This book will put you on the right path to completing your degree. Remember, it is never too late to learn.

Top Ten Reasons to Continue Your Education

---

10. **Fulfill a Dream—Or Begin One**
Make that wish a reality.

9. *Have Fun!*
There are plenty of opportunities for some great times.

8. **Make Connections that Can Link You to Future Jobs**
The friends, professors, and classmates you meet will provide valuable ties for future jobs and associations within the community.

7. **Become Part of a Cultural Stew**
Being in college is a good way to expose yourself to many types of people from various backgrounds and geographic locations, with different viewpoints and opinions. You may discover that you like things you never knew existed.

6. **Meet New People**
By furthering your education, you will widen your circle of friends.

5. **Do What You Love Doing and Get Paid For It**
This is what happens when you combine education and training with the right job. Work becomes more like play, which is far more satisfying and rewarding.

4. **Increase Your Sense of Personal Accomplishment**
Exercise your mind—mental exercise keeps your mind free of cobwebs. Education holds the key to the most interesting and challenging information you can imagine. Explore your outer limits and become a lifelong learner.

3. **Advance In Your Career and Earn a Higher Income**
Although money isn't everything, it is necessary for survival. A good education prepares you to become a solid member of society.

2. **Learn Critical-Thinking and Analytical Skills**
Furthering your learning will help you to think critically, organize and analyze information, and write clearly.

1. **Ensure That You Won't Get Left Behind**
In the next decade, you will need to learn new skills in order to keep up with changes in industry, communications, and technology. Education and training will give you a solid background. It will enable you to perform any occupation at a higher level of proficiency and professionalism.

Kinds of Colleges

Universities

A university is simply this: a large college. It is often state-supported and can be defined as containing several colleges, such as the College of Law, the College of Liberal Arts, or the College of Sciences.

Universities offer the following degrees:

- **Four-Year Degree**

  This is either a Bachelor of Arts (B.A.) or a Bachelor of Science (B.S.). It is also called a baccalaureate degree and consists of 120 to 136 semester hours of credit or its quarter-hour equivalent.

- **Master's Degree**

  This requires one or two years of academic credit past the bachelor's and usually results in either a Master of Arts (M.A.) or Master of Science (M.S.). It may or may not require a thesis. There are many variations as well, such as the Master of Business Administration (M.B.A.) and the Master of Fine Arts (M.F.A.)

- **Doctoral Degree**

  This is the highest academic award a student can earn for graduate study. It is offered by many universities and usually results in a Ph.D. (Doctor of Philosophy) in a particular academic field. For example, you could earn a Ph.D. in math, history, engineering, or public administration. It requires three or more years of graduate work beyond a master's degree and completion of a dissertation approved by faculty committee.

■ **Professional Degree** This degree is specific to a certain profession, such as medicine, law, pharmacy, optometry, theology, and veterinary medicine. It requires (1) completion of academic requirements to begin practice in the profession, (2) at least two years of college work prior to entering the program, and (3) a total of at least six academic years of college work to complete the degree program, including prior college work plus the length of the professional program itself.

In some cases, you should consider applying directly to a university. An alternative is to transfer to a university after you have completed two years at a community college. Generally, your two years of work will be accepted toward the bachelor's degree if you have planned your curriculum carefully during your freshman and sophomore years.

Colleges

Colleges tend to be smaller than universities, have a more restricted range of offerings, and are often specialized.

■ **Liberal Arts Colleges**
Liberal arts colleges offer degrees with concentrations of study in such fields as psychology, history, politics, philosophy, literature, foreign languages, fine arts, and so forth.

■ **Scientific or Technical Colleges**
Scientific or technical colleges offer degrees with concentrations of study in such fields as mathematics, physics, engineering, astronomy, architecture, and so forth.

■ **Vocational Schools and Colleges**
Vocational schools and colleges train students in a highly specific career field such as commercial illustration, accounting, advertising, real estate, insurance, cosmetology, journalism, film making, acting, and so forth. Most are

private and profitmaking, therefore, the tuition may be high. The entire course of study is often two years or less. Many vocational colleges are accredited, but many others have degrees not recognized by other colleges. Be on guard and thoroughly research a vocational college before attending it.

- **Community Colleges**

  Community colleges are usually fully accredited two-year institutions supported by a combination of state funds and local taxes. They offer a two-year program leading to either an Associate of Arts (A.A.) or an Associate of Science (A.S.) degree. The student who earns an associate degree can go on to complete a bachelor's degree in two more years at a four-year institution. See the *Community Colleges* section in this book for additional information.

Additional Resources

These Peterson's books can be found in any major bookstore or college bookstore:

Four-Year Colleges
Two-Year Colleges
Christian Colleges & Universities
College & University Almanac
Culinary Schools
Guide to Career Colleges
Law Schools
MBA Programs
Nursing Programs
Professional Degree Programs in the Visual and
*   Performing Arts*
Vocational and Technical Schools East
Vocational and Technical Schools West

Community Colleges

• Why Go to a Community College?

"Community" colleges do just that: they serve their communities. A community college is a two-year institution whose students are mostly commuters. Community colleges do not house students in dorms, fraternities, or sororities.

• What Are the Strengths of a Community College?

- There are smaller class sizes.
- You can attend part-time. A large percentage of community college students work full- or part-time.
- The college is probably small enough that you can get special attention.
- The tuition is lower than tuition at a four-year college. Legal residents of the state and military personnel stationed in that state usually pay less than nonresidents.
- It is easier to be admitted, since there are no admission tests. A high school diploma or equivalent is the main admission requirement.

• Community Colleges Have Three Types of Programs

1. College Preparatory or Precollege Programs

Not all of the students who enter community college are writing, reading, or doing math at a college level. So, most community colleges test incoming students in these areas. If you need a brush up or review, you can get it at your community college.

2. Vocational Programs

Most community colleges offer two-year vocational programs that lead directly into the job market. Many colleges are known for certain types of these programs. For example, some community colleges specialize in the biomedical field, computer technology, culinary arts, drafting, automotive, and so on. Check out the vocational programs at your community college. See if one of the fields interests you, especially if you are undecided about what kind of education you want and what you will do with it.

When you complete a vocational program, you receive an Associate of Applied Science (A.A.S.) degree. An A.A.S. cannot be used to transfer to a four-year university or college.

3. College Transfer Programs

A large number of students are enrolled in community colleges to get the first two years of their college career in a smaller, less stressful environment that is more economical. If you fall into this category, here are some quick tips:

- Plan out your classes for your freshman and sophomore years to ensure you meet all the requirements.

- Make sure you are enrolling in transferable classes.

- Check out the transfer agreements between your college and the universities in the area.

- Get in touch with the university where you want to transfer and find out about any unusual requirements.

When you complete a college transfer program, you earn an Associate of Science (A.S.) or an Associate of Arts (A.A.) degree. Note that even if you are planning to transfer to a four-year college for your Bachelor of Arts (B.A.) degree, you still may want to consider an A.A. or an A.S. degree. It is great for putting on a resume or job application. Check out the requirements for an associate degree and then decide if you want to try to meet those requirements. Some students opt to transfer to start working toward their bachelor's degree and skip the associate degree.

What Should You Take Advantage of While You Are at a Community College?

Save Money for a Rainy Day

You are spending far less on a comparable education. Be aware of it! Save now, so you will have a cushion when you need it, perhaps while pursuing a more expensive education.

Take Advantage of Smaller Classes and Smaller Student-Teacher Ratios

Community colleges are known as teaching, not research, institutions. The instructors are hired to teach, not bury themselves in the library. You will have small classes in the 25- to 35-students range. These classes are taught by instructors who want to teach you; get to know them. Take classes from the instructors you like, and avoid the ones you don't.

Meet Other Students

Community colleges have diverse student bodies. Make an effort to meet the students in your classes. Form study groups. Learn about other cultures. Listen to the experiences of people who have been out there longer than you have.

Additional Resources

These Peterson's books can be found in any major bookstore or college bookstore:

> *Two-Year Colleges*
> *Guide to Career Colleges*

Accreditation Overview

What is Accreditation, and Why Is It Important?

The accreditation status of a college, university, or vocational institution gives you an indication of its general quality. It means that the school has undergone an in-depth review, met certain standards, and is found worthy of approval. Accreditation is performed by independent, nongovernmental agencies. It assists students in making decisions by identifying schools worthy of investment.

Seeking accreditation is entirely voluntary on the part of the institution. The initial accreditation process takes a long time—from two to six years or more—and it costs money. Most legitimate accrediting agencies require the school to be in operation for at least a few years before they begin the accreditation process. Being awarded candidacy status does not ensure that an institution will eventually be fully accredited.

There are many unrecognized or phony accrediting agencies. So if a school says it's accredited, the key question is "Accredited by whom?" The best advice to any person is to attend a school accredited by an accrediting body recognized by the U. S. Department of Education (USDE).

Types of Accreditation

There are three basic types of recognized accreditation:

1. Regional Accreditation

Regional accreditation is awarded to an institution by one of six regional accrediting agencies, each of which covers a specified portion of the United States and its territories. They are Middle States, New England, North Central, Northwest, Southern, and Western.

If a college or university is regionally accredited, that means the institution as a whole has met the accrediting agency's standards. Most four-year universities, public and private, as well as two-year community colleges are regionally accredited.

2. National Accreditation

National accreditation is awarded to primarily private, for-profit schools that offer a wide diversity of subject matter and are national in their activities. There are sixteen national accrediting bodies, e.g., the Distance Education and Training Council (DETC), the Accrediting Commission for Career Schools and Colleges of Technology (ACCST), the Council on Occupational Education (COE), and the Accrediting Association of Bible Colleges (AABC).

3. Specialized Accreditation

Specialized accreditation (sometimes called professional accreditation) applies to a single department or program within a larger institution of higher education, or it can apply to a school that only provides training in one specific field. The accredited unit may be as big as a college within a university or as small as a curriculum within a field of study. There are specialized/professional accrediting agencies in about fifty-five fields, including acupuncture, health sciences, cosmetology, art and design, Bible college education, engineering, law, marriage and family therapy, nursing, and teacher education.

In some professional fields, you must have a degree or certificate from an accredited school or program in order to take qualifying exams or practice the profession.

What Does Accreditation Mean to You?

There are several benefits of enrolling in a regionally accredited college or university:

- You are assured of a basic level of quality education and services.

- Credits you earn are more likely to be transferable to other regionally accredited institutions, although each institution makes its own decisions on transfer credits on a case-by-case basis.

- Any certificate or degree you earn is more likely to be recognized by employers as a legitimate credential.

- You may qualify for federal loans and grants because regionally accredited institutions, like nationally accredited institutions, are eligible to participate in federal financial aid programs.

Checking on a School and Its Accreditors

It's important to find out what role accreditation plays in your field, since it may affect your professional future as well as the quality of your education.

So how can you tell if the school or college in which you are interested is accredited by an accrediting agency recognized by the U.S. Department of Education?

- If you are a Service member, contact your local military education center. There are counselors at these centers who are familiar with accreditation. Their main reference book is the *Accredited Institutions of Post-Secondary Education,* published by the American Council on Education. It lists all accrediting agencies recognized by the Department of Education and the schools accredited by these agencies.

- Check the U.S. Department of Education Web site. It has a complete list of recognized accrediting agencies. See http://www.ed.gov/offices/OPE/accreditation/natlagencies. html

Additional Points to Remember

- "Licensed by the state" and accredited are two different things. Some schools advertise that they are licensed by the state to blur the distinction between being licensed and having accreditation. All schools must have a license to operate; in some states, this is similar to a business license, meaning that all the school must do is fill out paperwork; other states have more rigorous requirements for licensure.

- If a school indicates it's accredited, make sure you identify the accrediting agency. It may be an agency that is unrecognized, insincere, or nonexistent.

- A school that indicates it's approved for GI Bill benefits is NOT necessarily accredited. The VA approves both accredited and nonaccredited institutions. They use a different set of criteria to approve schools.

What Is Distance Learning?

Distance education enables you to access education without having to physically be in a classroom on a campus. Various technologies are used to deliver courses to off-campus sites, to the workplace, and to your home.

• Why Should You Consider A Distance Learning Course or Degree Program?

To meet prerequisites, accelerate degree completion, complete courses not conducted locally, complete courses when travel or job obligations prevent class attendance, gain personal enrichment and satisfaction, excel in your current occupation, or prepare for a second career. Distance learning is for some the PREFERRED method of learning.

y want 2 do it

• Who Is A Good Distance Learning Student?

It's a person who has:

academic and emotional maturity.

specific goals.

the ability to work alone.

persistence and patience.

high reading and writing skills.

an academic support system from the school and a support system at home.

motivation and self-confidence.

Who Offers Distance Learning?

Traditional colleges, universities, graduate schools, community colleges, technical schools, and vocational schools.

The five most common subjects taught by distance education are

1. social sciences
2. business
3. education
4. computer science
5. health.

Schools have formed partnerships with cable companies, public broadcasting services, satellite broadcasters, and online education companies to deliver education.

How Does Distance Learning Work?

It may simply involve filling out a registration form, getting access to the equipment needed, and paying the tuition and fees. You may not need entrance examinations or proof of prior educational experience.

Other courses may have prerequisites. Some institutions offer a course outline upon request. You can review course descriptions and catalogs at the institution's home page on the Web.

What Type of Programs Are Available?

Credit Programs

If credit courses are completed successfully, they may be applied toward a degree.

Noncredit Programs

If you take a course on a noncredit basis, you may earn continuing education units (CEUs). One CEU is defined as 10 contact hours of participation in an organized class.

Professional Certification Programs

These programs help you acquire specialized knowledge in a specific field. They prepare you for a new career or professional licensure and certification. Many university programs are created in cooperation with professional and trade associations so that courses are based on real-life workforce needs.

How Can I Take Distance Learning Courses?

Colleges and universities collaborate with online information services, such as America Online, cable, and telephone companies, to provide education to far-flung students. Professions such as law, medicine, and accounting, as well as knowledge-based industries, use telecommunications networks to transmit education programs to working professionals.

What Are the Course Categories?

Print-Based Courses

Print-based courses are commonly called correspondence courses. Students receive materials by mail at the start of the course and return completed assignments by mail. Fax machines are used, and telephone calls can be made between instructor and student.

Audio-Based Courses

Audio-based courses involve two-way communication, as in audio or phone conferencing, or they involve one-way communication, including radio broadcast and prerecorded audiotapes.

Two-Way Interactive Video

Two-way interactive video courses take place simultaneously in two or more sites. The instructor is located in the home site with a group of students, and other students are located at satellite sites. Each site has TV monitors or large screens on which the instructor and students are viewed.

The course is conducted as a lecture. Students press a button on an apparatus on their desks when they wish to speak, which makes the camera point to them; their voices are transmitted to the other location. Quizzes and exams are faxed to the satellite site and faxed back or mailed by an assistant.

Prerecorded Video

Prerecorded video courses are videotaped and mailed to off-site students. The course may have a Web site where notes and assignments are posted. If students have questions, they can call or e-mail the instructor.

Internet-Based

Internet-based courses are also called online courses or e-learning. Some take place at specific times via interactive computer conferencing or chat rooms. Most occur at flexible times, making use of Web sites, e-mail, electronic mailing lists, newsgroups, bulletin boards, and messaging programs.

In courses offered at flexible times, instructors post instructional material and assignments on the course Web site. They start online discussions by posting a comment or question; students log on using a password and join the discussion at their convenience.

Students must have a computer with the appropriate software and Internet access to take an Internet-based course. Because the course material stays online for a period of time, students can log on at their own convenience.

To help ensure that students keep up, many instructors set weekly deadlines for reading lectures and completing assignments, require group projects, and make participation in online discussions mandatory.

Mixed Technologies

Mixed Technologies is a combination of technologies with print materials. A course can begin with a videoconference. A printed study guide is distributed to all participants at the first session. Students who cannot get to a videoconferencing site are sent a videocassette of the first session along with the study guide.

After the first session, the course moves online. Participants do their assignments and group projects while interacting online. Assignments are mailed to the instructor. The class concludes with another videoconference or recorded videotape.

How Do I Communicate With My Instructor?

Through fax, e-mail, and toll-free numbers. Interaction with your instructor—whether by computer, phone, or letter—is important, and you must take the initiative. •

What Are the Future Trends of Distance Learning?

Colleges and universities plan to increase their use of Internet-based instruction and two-way interactive video. Prerecorded video is likely to decrease in popularity.

The explosive growth in distance learning has come primarily from online courses, and that is likely to continue.

Selecting the Right Distance Learning Program

Here is a short guide of what to look for:

- **Curriculum**
  Make sure the curriculum meets your educational and professional goals.

- **Reputation**
  Consider the reputation of a university in general.

- **Academic Quality**
  Find out whether or not it is accredited by a specialized agency—if that applies in your field (see the article on accreditation).

- **Faculty**
  Check out the credentials of the faculty members. For academic programs, find out whether tenure-track professors with Ph.D.'s teach both on-campus and distance courses or if distance courses are relegated to part-time adjunct faculty members and/or assistants.

Experience with Adult Learners
Working adult students have different needs than full-time on-campus students.

The Technology

Find out what technical support is offered to students. The best setup is free technical support accessed via a toll-free number 24 hours a day, seven days a week.

Faculty-Student Interaction

Pay particular attention to the faculty-student ratio in online courses. If there are more than 25 to 30 students per instructor, you're not likely to get much individual attention.

Advising and Other Services

Check what advising services are offered to distance learners, and see how easy they are to access.

Time Frames

Check how much time you have to complete a certificate or degree program, and decide whether it meets your needs.

Cost

The cost is often the same for on-campus and distance students. If you enroll in a consortium, member institutions may charge tuition at different rates. Some institutions charge an extra technology fee to cover the costs associated with distance education.

Additional Resources

This Peterson's book can be found in any major bookstore, college bookstore, or military education center:

Guide to Distance Learning Programs

Surviving Standardized Tests

A Few Facts

Three major standardized tests students take are the SAT I and II, ACT Assessment, and CLEP. Colleges across the country use them to get a sense of a student's readiness for admission or to place them in appropriate courses. These are not intelligence tests; they are reasoning tests designed to evaluate the way you think. They assess the basic knowledge and skills you have gained through your classes in school and through outside experience.

Here are answers to some commonly asked questions.

Q: **What Is the ACT Assessment?**

A: The ACT Assessment is a standardized college entrance examination that measures knowledge and skills in four sections: English, mathematics, reading, and science reasoning. Each section is scored from 1 to 36 and is scaled for slight variations in difficulty. Students are not penalized for incorrect responses. The composite score is the average of the four scaled scores.

Q: **What Is the SAT I?**

A: The SAT I measures developed verbal and mathematical reasoning abilities as they relate to successful performance in college. It supplements the secondary school record and other information about the student in assessing readiness for college. It is a 3-hour test with seven sections, primarily multiple-choice, that measures verbal and mathematical abilities. The three verbal sections test vocabulary, verbal reasoning, and critical reading skills. Emphasis is placed on reading passages, which are 400–850 words in length. The three mathematics sections test a student's ability in arithmetic, algebra, and geometry. Calculators may be used on the mathematics sections.

Q: Should I Take the ACT or the SAT I?

A: It depends on the college you plan to attend. Some colleges accept the results of one test and not the other. Some institutions use test results for proper placement of students in English and math courses.

Q: What Are the SAT II Subject Tests?

A: Subject Tests are required by some institutions for admission and/or placement in freshman-level courses.

They are 1-hour tests, primarily multiple-choice, in specific subjects that measure students' knowledge of these subjects and their ability to apply that knowledge. The Subject Tests measure a student's academic achievement in high school and may indicate readiness for certain college programs.

College-Level Examination Program (CLEP)

The CLEP enables students to earn college credit for what they already know, whether it was learned in school, through independent study, or through experiences outside of the classroom. More than 2,800 colleges and universities now award credit for qualifying scores on one or more of the thirty-four CLEP exams. The exams are 90 minutes, primarily multiple-choice, and are administered at participating colleges and universities and at Military Education Centers worldwide.

How Do I Prepare for These Tests?

You should review relevant material, such as math formulas and commonly tested vocabulary words, and know the directions for each question type or test section. You should take at least one practice test and review your mistakes. There are study guides for these tests in every major commercial and college bookstore, and information can be found at the following Web sites:

> **ACT**—http://www.act.org
>
> **CLEP**—http://www.collegeboard.com
>
> **SAT**—http://www.ets.org

Visit http://www.petersons.com for resources on a variety of standardized tests.

Additional Resources

These Peterson's and ARCO books can be found in any major bookstore or college bookstore:

> *ACT Success (Peterson's)*
> *Master the ACT (ARCO)*
> *SAT Success (Peterson's)*
> *Master the SAT (ARCO)*
> *30 Days to the SAT (ARCO)*
> *CLEP Success (Peterson's)*
> *Master the CLEP (ARCO)*

Choosing Classes

Fifteen Tips on Choosing Classes

1. Don't Overburden Yourself

Don't take a gigantic course load. At the same time, don't take such a light course load that you won't be challenged.

2. Don't Sign Up for Three Reading-Intensive Courses

Try to vary the type of courses you take. Balance your class load between courses with a lot of reading and courses that have problem sets.

Math and science courses include biology, chemistry, physics, and geometry; these classes will usually have problem sets for homework.

Humanities or reading-intensive courses include classes in anthropology, English, history, political science, psychology, and various other social sciences.

3. Sample a Variety of Subject Areas

It's okay to be leaning toward a specific major, but don't rule out other subject areas without giving them a chance.

Subjects you enjoyed in high school may not interest you in college. You may find academic happiness in a totally random subject area. Come to college with an open mind; you can always switch back to original academic plans at a later date.

4. Choose Professors, Not Titles

A professor makes a course—not the other way around. Find out who the best professors are and take their classes, especially if they are in your field. Try to get into classes with the best teachers.

5. Get Your Requirements Out of the Way Early

Most schools have general education requirements that make it mandatory for each student to take courses in a variety of areas. It's a great way to sample various fields. They often turn out to be interesting courses, which may lead your education in a totally different direction.

6. If You Have Problems, Seek Human (Not Computer) Assistance

Many larger schools are now letting students register via the Internet or automated telephone. While these methods often simplify the process, don't hesitate to call the registrar's office if you have a problem. This applies to any concerns with registration. Don't wait until classes start to figure out that you are not enrolled in any.

7. Don't Worry About A Major Just Yet

Nobody will be asking you to declare a major as soon as you get to college. As a matter of fact, most advisers will discourage it.

You need to answer many questions before choosing a major. What kind of job are you planning on? Do you wish to attend graduate school? What interests you?

These questions can be answered after your freshman courses, after you have decided what you like, and after you have figured out the subjects in which you excel.

Keep in mind that your major does not necessarily dictate your future career.

8. Read Your College Catalog

It contains: (a) required courses, (b) majors offered and curriculums to follow, and (c) course prerequisites and descriptions.

9. Make Sure You Discuss with Your Academic Adviser and Understand the Issue of TRANSFERABILITY of Course Work

To talk with that person, first make an appointment. Be prepared by being familiar with the catalog.

10. Find Out If You Must Take A Refresher Course

Many colleges require placement tests in English and math. The results will indicate whether you must take a refresher course BEFORE beginning freshman-level courses. Refresher courses are usually numbered 0-100. You receive credit for them, but they do NOT transfer to other institutions.

11. Improve Your Writing Skills

Take an English refresher course if necessary. Learning to write term papers and themes will be a major task in college, but your reward will be a VALUABLE LIFETIME ASSET. Exams, research papers, and term papers will be evaluated on grammar, punctuation, clarity, organization, logic, creativity, and your ability to gather, analyze, and communicate knowledge successfully.

12. If You Withdraw From A Class, Make Sure You Do It Within the Official "Add-Drop" Period

Otherwise, if you just quit going to class without notifying the school, you will receive an "F." If you withdraw within the official "Add-Drop" period, you usually can receive a refund or partial refund from the school. Regardless of the reason, ALWAYS fill out the official withdrawal papers.

13. Take A Speech Class

Speaking effectively is a MAJOR advantage in today's world.

14. Put It in Writing!

An academic adviser or dean may give you permission to take an advanced course or waive a degree requirement, but at graduation, that person may no longer be at the college. Any exceptions granted you from the published procedures should be noted in writing and placed in your permanent file.

15. Make Sure You Fulfill Your School's Residency Requirement

This means you must complete a certain number of courses with the school from which you're seeking a degree. Some schools require the last year of college work to be done in residence. The residency requirement may be 15 semester hours for an associate degree and 30 semester hours for a bachelor's degree.

Study Tactics

Classwork: What to Expect

The days when teachers looked over your shoulder and nagged you about homework and tests are gone. Teachers assume you can keep up with your work without individual attention.

The structure of college courses reflects this philosophy. Instead of daily graded assignments and monthly tests, most college professors evaluate students solely on the basis of two or three assessments—most probably, a midterm, final, term project, or several papers.

Just as often, the professor will not say anything about assignments but rely on the syllabus given to each student the first day of class. This item—the syllabus—is invaluable; keep it in a safe place.

With class work structured in this way, falling behind haunts any student with the slightest lazy streak. The laid-back student may find himself approaching the midterm or even the final without having read or written anything. Time management plays a large role in your college career.

Homework: How to Stay on Top

Self-discipline and organization are the keys.

Plot Your Time With A Calendar

Set daily and weekly goals. Study daily. Learn to take careful notes.

Expect to spend at least two nights studying for any significant exam. Papers may require more time if research is needed—sometimes you may need to order books from another library, and that could set you back a few days. And don't make the mistake of waiting until 5 minutes before a paper is due to print it out. Inevitably, the printer will jam when you need it most.

Don't get behind in your other classes while concentrating on one.

Attend Class

College professors assume students are disciplined enough to attend class on a regular basis. Class attendance is critical to college success.

Copying notes from a more disciplined friend will not suffice. Notes should be used as an outline, reminding you of key concepts and theories. Borrowed notes will give you facts and figures but won't paint the complete picture.

If you have time, read your lecture notes at the end of each day or at least the end of the week.

Review, rewrite, and discuss classwork. The more you work with the material, the more you will remember.

Learn How to Study Effectively

First, find a suitable study environment. Some like soft music in the background. Some need people around. For most, however, a comfortable chair in a quiet room works best. Regardless, make sure you are in a place free of the temptation to socialize.

- Don't study in bed.

- Use breaks as incentives. A good rule is to work for 50 minutes and break for 10.

- Remember to highlight important points in the chapters you read. It makes studying before an exam so much easier.

Procrastination: Avoid the Inevitable

At one time or another, every college student will get behind in his or her work—no matter how disciplined or diligent the person. Although the struggle to stay afloat in the sea of academia challenges every student, it should not be an excuse to drown.

Keep Up with Your Reading

Review—review—review.

Do Not Plagiarize

This means do not write a paper with words you took from another source. Your writing must be your own. There are now computer programs available to professors that can detect plagiarism.

Maintain A High Grade Point Average (GPA)

Grades of "D" and "F" will not transfer to another institution. If you have an "Incomplete," make up the required work in time to receive a passing grade; otherwise it will become an "F."

Learn How to Use the Library or Internet to Do Research

The more you know about where to find information in your library and on the Internet, the easier your research will be.

Keep Copies of All Assigned Projects, Term Papers, and Returned Tests

Keep them until you receive your grade at the end of the course.

Additional Resources

These Peterson's and ARCO books can be found in any major bookstore or college bookstore:

> *Essential Math for College-Bound Students*
> *Essential Vocabulary for College-Bound Students*
> *Reading Lists for College-Bound Students*
> *Triple Your Reading Speed*
> *In-a-Flash: Math*
> *In-a-Flash: Vocabulary*

How to Manage Time Well

It takes intelligence and a conscious effort to manage time well. Below are some of the skills involved.

- **Reflect On Your Age**

  Take on a new attitude toward it. Think of yourself as comparatively young no matter what your age.

- **Stop Taking On Too Much At Once**

  Limit your responsibilities and lighten your burden.

- **Learn to Cope With Your Own Personality**

  If you are high-strung and induce much of your own time pressure, decide that you don't have to be the victim of yourself.

- **Reject Perfectionism**

  Decide that you have a right to be imperfect. There *are* times to have high standards, to strive for excellence, but in order to protect your mental and emotional health, there are also times to say, "This is good enough."

- **Cope With Procrastination**

  If chronic procrastination is one of your problems, develop a strategy for coping with it.

- **Learn to Get An Early Start**

  This is largely under your control. Early starts provide you with a safety net.

- **Assign Priorities to Your Tasks**

  Don't feel guilty about tasks that you neglect for a few days because of more urgent demands.

- **Make A Rational Schedule**
  Design this to meet the needs of a typical week. Plan
  effectively and reduce details to their proper proportions.

Writing A Term Paper

Q: **What Is a Term Paper?**

A: A term paper is a relatively long report or essay on a specific topic. It is submitted to satisfy a course requirement.

Q: **Why Are Term Papers Assigned at All?**

A: Term papers are assigned to prove you can make connections between concepts, do research, synthesize and organize ideas, and express your thoughts in a clear form. It also helps the instructor evaluate your grasp of the subject.

Q: **What Kinds of Courses Require Term Papers?**

A: Term papers are likely to be required in social science and humanities courses. Examples include English literature, psychology, philosophy, anthropology, sociology, and history. A term paper is seldom required in life science or physical science courses such as biology, anatomy, physiology, astronomy, and physics. Term papers are seldom required in applied courses such as accounting, marketing, word processing, real estate, statistics, and business mathematics.

Q: **How Does a Term Paper Differ from a Thesis or a Dissertation?**

A: A term paper is much shorter than a thesis or a dissertation, which tend to resemble book-length manuscripts. A thesis is submitted to satisfy one of the requirements for a master's degree, and a dissertation is submitted to satisfy one of the requirements for a doctoral degree.

Q: **But I've Heard That a Term Paper Must Have a Thesis. Can You Clarify?**

A: The term *thesis* can be used in two ways. To say that you are *writing* a thesis means you are writing a long report or essay for a master's degree. To say that your term paper must *have* a thesis means it must make a point; it must have some central idea. It is a good idea to set out this point or idea early in the paper. Then bring forth evidence that either supports or rejects it.

Q: **How Long Should a Term Paper Be?**

A: The ideal length for a term paper is about 3,000 to 3,500 words. This is 12 to 14 typewritten pages. Professors may provide you with the length required.

Q: **How Do You Do Research for a Term Paper?**

A: Learn to use the library's reference resources. A card or computer catalog will list many subjects. Look up the subject you have picked and then find books and articles that contain information on your topic. The indexes and bibliographies of the books and articles will often suggest other sources. If your library doesn't have a particular publication, request it through an interlibrary loan. There are also helpful publications for researchers, such as *Books in Print* and *The Reader's Guide to Periodical Literature*. In addition, there are annual abstracts published for some subjects, such as *Psychological Abstracts*.

Another source of information is the Internet. You can do a search by the subject name of your paper and find links to

Web sites containing information for your paper. Be sure to cite your sources as you would cite book sources.

It is important that you cite primary sources as well as secondary ones in a term paper. A *primary source* of information is a "first," or basic, source. A *secondary source* of information is one that has been derived from primary ones.

Q: How Do I Put a Term Paper into a Proper Form?

A: Obtain *A Manual for Writers of Term Papers, Theses, and Dissertations,* written by Kate L. Turabian and revised and expanded by Bonnie Birtwistle Honingsblum. It is published by the University of Chicago Press. The manual will show you how to make a table of contents, cite publications, organize a bibliography, and so forth. The bookstore will also have other good manuals available.

How to Find A Topic

First, it should not be too difficult to research or too broad in scope. Second, it should have an aspect that you can state in the form of a thesis. And third, the subject should excite some actual interest in you.

Open the course-assigned textbook to the index. Read the textbook entry for the subject, and that is your starting point. Use it as a stimulus for your own thought processes. Ask yourself how you could make an interesting statement about the topic, one that could be answered to some extent by library research. Then focus your research on information that sheds some light on the topic.

Using the Four Stages of Creative Thinking

There are four basic stages in creative thinking:

1. preparation
2. incubation
3. illumination
4. verification

For a concrete example of the four stages, let's turn to a sample term paper called "The Mild, Mild West" in which we assert that the Old West wasn't as wild as it has been said to have been.

Preparation

Perhaps you have read two or three Western novels by such authors as Zane Grey, Max Brand, or Louis L'Amour. Then, using the library's resources, find books and articles on the way people lived approximately 100 years ago in such states as Texas, Arizona, Nevada, and California. Read only the material pertinent to your topic. Use the bibliographies of the first books to suggest additional books and articles. Take plenty of notes. Put these on index cards of a standard size to arrange and rearrange your material. Also, make photocopies of key pages.

Incubation

Set aside your notes for a week or two. Incubation in creative thinking is a mental process involving learning and growth at a subconscious level. Although you do not give conscious attention to the subject matter, apparently some process of connecting between facts and ideas goes on outside your voluntary control. It is a very real phenomenon, one you can count on. Note that *time* is involved, however. Work on the term paper, including preparation and incubation, should be spread out over a three- to four-week period. For this reason, it is important to get an early start and not procrastinate.

Illumination

After the incubation period, come back to the material. You will be pleasantly surprised to find that it tends to organize itself easily, and you have some good ideas about how to write it. For example, you see that a gunfight from a Western novel can be quoted briefly in an introduction. This gets the paper off to an interesting start. The following four topical headings come naturally to mind:

1. The Popular View
2. A Realistic View
3. An Evaluation, and
4. A Personal Viewpoint.

Verification

The last step involves actually writing the term paper. You are verifying your ideas and your organization, turning mental musings into actual sentences and paragraphs on paper. Verification is a trial-and-error process. It is for good reason that a first draft is also called a *rough draft.* The key goal is to produce a document. After something is down on paper, it is relatively easy to go back over it two or three times, editing, rewriting, and improving the paper.

Specific Tips and Writing Strategies

- **Start Your Paper with An Example, A Quotation, or An Anecdote that Is Intrinsically Interesting and Attention Getting**

  This helps to lift your paper out of the pile of dull and uninspired term papers your instructor plows through at the end of each semester.

- **Keep the Writing Clear and To the Point**

  Use relatively short sentences ranging in length from ten to fourteen words. If a sentence has too many clauses and subclauses and approaches a length of twenty or more words, break it down into two shorter sentences. Use a vocabulary that is appropriate to your subject, but don't show off by using obscure words when more familiar, workable words will do.

- **Use Headings and Subheadings**

  Give your term paper about four or five main headings. Use subheadings if the material can be further categorized. Be sure you have at least two subheadings, if you use them at all, under a main heading. The use of headings and subheadings makes your paper appear logical and organized. Twelve pages of writing without headings can look like a big lump of indigestible mental oatmeal.

■ **Limit Your References**

Don't go overboard on research for a term paper. Remember, it is not a thesis or a dissertation. If your term paper is 12 pages in length, then 10 to 14 references will be about right. If you have too few references, your paper will not be adequately documented. If you have too many references, your paper will seem to be cluttered and written from index cards. Be sure you rely mainly on *primary* references of high quality.

■ **Summarize All References In A Bibliography**

A bibliography is a real showcase for your research. It is often the first item an instructor turns to, so be sure that it is neat, accurate, and presented in correct form; this will really help to move your paper up your professor's grading scale.

■ **Edit the Paper Carefully**

Double-check and triple-check your paper for spelling errors, grammar, and general syntax.

■ **Pay Attention to the Paper's General Appearance**

A whole grade point can often be gained or lost on a term paper because of its overall look. The best look is obtainable with the use of a laser printer. If you don't have adequate equipment, have your paper copied and run off at a modest cost by a professional service.

■ **Use Some Direct Quotations**

Direct quotations, properly referenced, lend weight and authority to your paper. Be sure they are interesting, insightful, and pertinent to the content. Three or four quotations here and there, in a standard-length term paper, are about the right number.

- **Remember that Writing Is Rewriting**
  Write the first draft relatively rapidly, and rewrite and edit
  at your leisure.

Additional Resources

These ARCO books can be found in any major bookstore or college
bookstore:

> *10,000 Ideas for Term Papers, Projects, Reports,*
> *and Speeches*
> *How to Write Research Papers*

Tips for Making A Presentation

Have An Attention-Getting Introduction

Try to think of some way to "hook" an audience. An anecdote, a clever quotation, a news item, or a reference to a celebrity are all examples of material that have interest built into them.

Make Eye Contact

Use the principle of *roving eye contact*. Make it, hold it for 20 or 30 seconds, and then move on to someone else at random. Make sure that you include people at the back.

Use A Visual Aid Or A Handout

A handout can be either an outline or a list of key questions that you plan to address. Members of an audience tend to cling to handouts.

Speak So You Can Be Heard

Some students insist on giving a talk in soft, whispery tones. This can come from anxiety. You are *supposed to be* the center of attention. Will yourself to speak up. A little too loud is better than a little too quiet.

Make Some Movements

Take a few steps forward or back once in a while. Change your position. Come out from behind the lectern for a few moments. Walk over to the blackboard. Point at your visual aid. Motion automatically commands attention. It involuntarily makes all eyes focus on the body in motion and brings the audience together.

Use Natural Hand Gestures

The appropriate "hand language" that comes naturally to you from your cultural background gives color and personality to what you have to say. Let your hands be spontaneously expressive.

Use A Key-Questions Format

Draw up a series of four to seven key questions. Read the first question to the group, then look up and answer the question informally. Proceed through the other questions in the same way. The key-questions format is effective because questions automatically alert the mind and induce a natural interest.

Talk With Feeling

Some students deliver a talk in a dull monotone. Often, their faces seem to go blank and they lack expression. Conversely, other students vary the pitch of their voices. Their eyes and facial expression convey feeling, a degree of emotional intensity. The content of two talks can be almost the same, but the one delivered with feeling and liveliness will go over far better with an audience.

Allow Some Time For A Question-And-Answer Period

It is always gracious and a courtesy to invite some questions from the audience. It also conveys the impression that you are the master of your material. No more than two or three questions need to be accepted. The quality of your answers is really not as important as the confidence with which you present them. Keep your answers relatively short. And, remember, in a question-and-answer format, you have a right to the last word. In your momentary role as speaker, you are the authority on the subject in question.

Additional Resources

These ARCO books can be found in any major bookstore or college bookstore:

> *How to Write and Deliver Effective Speeches*
> *10,000 Ideas for Term Papers, Projects, Reports,*
> *and Speeches*

Tips for Taking An Exam

Multiple-Choice Tests

- Be sure you answer every question. Go over the test and double-check.

- After you have completed the test, reevaluate the difficult questions and consider changing answers. You may pick up overall points from double-checking and making changes.

- Many answer sheets these days are machine graded. It is essential that all marks be dark and in accordance with instructions.

- Ask your instructor if you can use a standard dictionary. Often, looking up a single word will turn a difficult multiple-choice question into a clear one.

- If English is a second language for you, ask the instructor if you can bring in an English-foreign language dictionary. Don't hesitate to ask. This request is quite appropriate, and most instructors will agree to it.

- Study for multiple-choice tests by the recall method. Although a multiple-choice test is a recognition test, the general rule is this: *If you can recall an item, you can certainly recognize it.*

Essay Examinations

- Give your essay an organization. Don't just ramble and free associate. Decide what point or points you want to make and proceed to make them.

- Don't strive for a literary style. The purpose of an essay examination is to assess learning. Say what you need to say as directly and as clearly as possible.

- An essay question measures your grasp of basic information and your capacity for critical thinking. Try to work into the essay all of the relevant, specific ideas or facts that you can muster. Use terms and names and define concepts. Also, make connections between concepts. Tie ideas together.

- Make your essay a good length. An essay that is too short will seem to be a minimal, feeble effort. An essay that is too long will seem to be padded. Student essays that run over 1,000 words (about five to six handwritten pages) are usually too long. The typical student essay runs in the vicinity of 400 to 500 words. This is about two or three handwritten pages.

- Make your essay as presentable as possible. Pay attention to spelling and grammar. Write clearly and legibly. Factors such as these have an impact on the grade.

Six Quick Test-Taking Tips

1. Remember Partial Credit

Always show your work. If worse comes to worst, write *something* down, anything. Partial credit has salvaged more than a few test scores, especially in science courses where the median score is often 40 percent or lower.

2. Use Key Words and Catch Phrases

If your essay has a lot of these key words, you may earn an A or B; if not, you may receive a C or D.

3. Write Clearly

Write with clarity and purpose. The object is simple but contradictory: Get down as much as possible in the most logical fashion.

4. Always Agree

Unless you *really* know your stuff, don't disagree with the teacher. Regurgitation, however boring, is your best bet come grade time.

5. Answer Every Question, If Possible

Don't spend 2 hours answering the first question when you have five more of equal weight staring you in the face. Bide your time and make sure to answer most completely those questions that are worth the most points.

6. Don't Stress Out

Getting uptight because you can't answer the first question is useless. Move on. If the rest of the test looks like Chinese when it's supposed to be Spanish, do the best you can. Excessive worrying only makes you less productive.

Computers at College

Questions to Consider Before You Buy a Computer

Q: Do I Already Own An Adequate Computer System?

A: The computer world changes so fast that it is hard to say what an *adequate* system is. The best rule of thumb is that any computer system that is more than two or three years old is probably about to reach dinosaur status, and if you can afford it, you will want to replace such a system.

Q: Does the School Provide Sufficient Computer Facilities?

A: Many colleges offer easily accessible computer facilities. For the student on a tight budget, it pays to investigate. If the computer facilities at your school are particularly good, you may not need your own computer.

Q: What Type of Computer Do Most Students Use?

A: The most popular with students are IBM PC-compatible computers.

Q: **Does My Major Require A Special Computer?**

A: Engineering and computer science students may have special computer needs, whereas English and history majors may need to use only simple wordprocessing programs. A superexpensive Mac or IBM-compatible system may be overkill if all you have to do is crank out three papers a term and surf the Web.

Despite what you might think, you'll probably want your own computer as much for your English and history courses (to have privacy while you write) as your science courses (which may use computers for writing labs or statistical analysis).

Use and Abuse of Computers

Be Sure to Set Your Computer to Automatically Save Your Work Every 10 Minutes

These days, all word processing programs have a setting that allows you to program your machine to save your work automatically every few minutes. Make sure that you have the AutoSave function set.

If your computer does crash, don't panic! Your machine will probably recover your file when you reboot. If not, find a friend who knows how to access your "temp" files; it might be in there. You can also use the "find file" command and then limit the search to files that were recently updated. Get help if you need it, because chances are that your material is not all lost.

Keep Your Computer In A Cool Place and Away From Food

Computers located too close to a vent or radiator may decide to take the day off due to heat exhaustion. Soda pop, milk, and beer also have contributed to many a system's downfall. Magnets are a bad idea, too. Keep them far away from your computer and floppy disks.

Get to Know A Computer Guru

You know who they are. There is no magic involved—these folks really know what they're doing, and they're usually glad to help you out of a computer bind.

Keep Your Computer Running Smoothly

As an added precaution against breakdowns, have someone check up on your computer every year or so. Most computer service stores will do a diagnostic check for $30 to $40. It might save some hassles later.

Protect Against Viruses

Be careful when you borrow floppy disks or download material via the Web. You should make sure that your computer is equipped with good virus protection software. The newer the software, the more viruses it will be able to recognize.

Don't Let the Computer Become An Enemy

Don't let that little glowing screen become an adversary. If you plan correctly and take all the necessary precautions, the computer will be your most useful tool at college—next to your brain.

Internet Glossary

Browser A type of software that allows you to research the World Wide Web, such as Netscape's Navigator and Communicator programs or Microsoft's Internet Explorer. Browsers assemble all the elements of Web pages to form a clear, coherent display.

Directories These make sense of the Internet's clamor by sorting and organizing information according to specific categories, such as Education, News, or Entertainment. Yahoo! is a popular directory.

Home Page   This is the welcome mat for a Web site. It is usually the first page you see, and it could well be the only page. For bigger sites with lots of information, the home page functions as an index, telling you what else is on the site, with links to whisk you there.

HTML   HyperText Markup Language. The computer language used to build Web pages.

Internet   A massive public computer network of smaller computer networks linked globally by high-speed telephone lines. The Internet's reach includes networks of colleges and universities, banks, insurance companies, museums, government agencies, movie studios, zoos, and much more.

Link   A connection to another Web site. Usually, you click on an underlined word or graphic to connect to the new site.

Search Engine   Similar to a directory, but it searches for data when you provide key words.

Server   A computer linked to the Internet that stores Web pages and responds to data requests.

Service Provider   An organization or company that provides a connection to the Internet through its host computer.

URL   Uniform Resource Locator. An address identifying a file location on the Internet.

World Wide Web   A navigation system that lets you browse and retrieve text, graphics, video, and sound from a variety of linked sources. Many people think the Web and the Internet are one and the same. They are not.

Web Resources for Students

Web Sites

A+ RESEARCH AND WRITING (http://www.ipl.org/teen/aplus).
Contains tips on how to write a research paper.

BARTLEBY.COM (http://www.bartleby.com/reference/). Has excellent references, such as *American Heritage Dictionary, Roget's Thesaurus, Elements of Style,* and *Bartlett's Quotations.*

BRITANNICA.COM (http://www.britannica.com). Plug in any subject, get articles and related Web sites.

COMMUNITY COLLEGE WEB (http://www.mcli.dist.maricopa.edu/cc/info.html). Contains a searchable index to & links to the Web sites for more than 1260 community colleges in the U.S., Canada, & elsewhere around the world.

DISTANCE LEARNING COLLEGES (http://www.CollegeDegree.com). A directory of degrees, certificates & courses offered through distance learning.

GOOGLE (http://www.google.com). A great all-purpose search engine on the Web.

GUIDE TO SEARCH ENGINES (http://www.unf.edu/library/guides/search.html). Put together by the University of North Florida.

INTERNET RESOURCES FOR MATH STUDENTS (http://www.langara.bc.ca/mathstats/resource/onWeb). This site has quick tutorials and online classes.

THE INTERNET PUBLIC LIBRARY (http://www.ipl.org). Great site to start research. Has reference, newspaper, and magazine links. Also contains archives of academic papers and tutorials on how to improve writing.

MIND EDGE (http://www.mindedge.com). A portal to search for distance learning or on-campus courses—academic, professional, continuing education, personal development. Includes corporate training courses as well.

NATIONAL GEOGRAPHIC.COM (http://www.nationalgeographic.com). Great source for biology and environment students.

PETERSONS.COM (http://www.petersons.com). Great source for information for choosing both undergraduate and graduate schools, distance learning programs, careers, and much more. Also a source for financial aid and scholarship information. Includes information and test prep for SAT, ACT, GRE, GMAT, ASVAB, and more.

PETERSON'S DISTANCE LEARNING (http://www.petersons.com/dlearn). Provides detailed information about distance learning programs offered by U.S. colleges & universities.

STUDENT SUCCESS SITE (http://www.prenhall.com/success/). Features to help students through their lifelong educational journey.

Online College Bookstores

BookSwap: http://www.bookswap.com

Barnes and Noble: http://www.barnesandnoble.com/textbooks

Efollet: http://www.efollett.com

ecampus.com: http://ecampus.com

TextSwap: http://www.textswap.com

StudentMarket: http://www.studentmarket.com

Ten Myths About College

1. College Is Only for Unusually Bright People

College students do not need to be "gifted," superior, or have unusual mental abilities. Most college graduates are perfectly ordinary people in terms of memory, attention span, arithmetical understanding, comprehension of concepts, and other abilities.

2. College Is Only for Unusually Creative People

The last thing required in most college classes is creativity. You need to learn in college, not invent or create ideas.

3. You Have to Be Young to Go to College

If you are 25 years or older, you will have plenty of companionship. At state universities and community colleges, older adults are the rule, not the exception. The average age of a part-time evening student is 29.

4. You Have to Have a Lot of Free Time to Go to College

It is best, when attending college part time, to take only two or three classes. If the class schedule is arranged in terms of your work or family responsibilities, you can generally find times and places to study.

5. It Takes a Lot of Money to Go to College

The average community college is subsidized by state and local taxes, so fees are relatively low. If money is very tight, you can consult the college's financial aid office. There are both grants and loans available to most students. Those in the military can use in-service VA education benefits and/or military tuition assistance.

6. It Takes a Long, Long Time to Complete a College Program

By going part time, it can take you longer to earn a degree. However, many schools have accelerated terms, allow students to earn credit by taking examinations such as the College Level Examination Program (CLEP), and award those who are or have been in the military with credit for their job experience and military training. Many community colleges also offer certificate programs in trade and vocational areas, which can be completed in less than the equivalent of two full-time years.

7. You Have to Pass Entrance Examinations in Order to Go to College

Although high scores on standardized examinations such as the Scholastic Assessment Tests (SAT I and II) are required for admission to some state universities and selective private colleges, this is not true of community colleges. Many colleges and universities on military installations do not require entrance examinations.

The majority of community colleges have an *open door* policy, meaning that all applicants are welcome. If you do your first two years of college work toward a bachelor's degree at a community college, your work can transfer to a four-year college or university without entrance examinations.

8. You Need to Know What You Want

If you don't know what area you want to pursue, declare something general such as liberal arts. If you are aiming toward a bachelor's degree, the first two years are general education courses. In most cases it is not necessary to take more than two or three courses in your major in your first two years. You can change your major readily after you complete your first two years.

Many students use the first two years of college as a way of *discovering* what they want to major in.

9. Professors Tend to Be Hostile to the Older, Nontraditional Student

The great majority of college professors look upon their work as not merely a job but as a high calling. Teachers live to teach. They want to help you succeed. If you demonstrate a genuine will to learn, the professor will usually find this both exciting and rewarding.

10. College Graduates Don't Really Earn That Much More Money Than Non-College Graduates

The average college graduate earns about twice as much money per year than the average high school graduate.

NOTES

NOTES

NOTES